The 30 Day
God Challenge

Setting Up For Success

The 30 Day God Challenge is designed to help you incorporate spiritual habits, often referred to as spiritual disciplines, into your daily and weekly life. For years world religions including Christianity have emphasized the importance of regular and consistent spiritual communion with God. In today's hustle and bustle world, finding God-time can be challenging, but for that reason it is also all the more crucial.

This book is not intended to be a "salvation" piece. I do not go into the effectiveness of prayer, why attending church is important and the wonderful benefits of a giving life style. This book is the step after. You know God and you are doing some of the things listed in this book already, but you are ready to deepen that relationship and seek to have more of him in your everyday life. You're ready for the challenge.

As you already know, repetition is the best teacher and the key to changing behavior. As you progress through the challenge, you will see check boxes to help you monitor your progress. If you miss something, don't worry, just keep going. You are developing new habits and like any habit, it will take time. You will notice that the prayer component starts with once a day the first week, twice a day the second week and three times a day to the finish. Feel free to pray more often, start with three-a-day if you think you can keep it up. Remember, consistency is more important than quantity, thus your prayer need not be lengthy.

As you move through the book chronologically, here are a few more thoughts and tips to help you get the most out of your experience.

1. When doing your daily devotion, find a quiet place with no distractions if possible.

2. On the Sundays you go to church, take the book with you to fill in your worship notes. This is not limited to preaching. Be open to God speaking through any aspect of the service.

3. For your kind gesture, find someone least suspecting. You both will be surprised!

4. I am not concerned about how much your offering is, but more with how consistent your giving is. We can talk about tithing later, right now we are developing the "habit" of giving. Give.

5. Say your thank you statement out loud. If you want a challenge bonus, say it to someone else. Don't under estimate this powerful gesture, especially when you are having a tough day.

I am praying your success and I honor your desire to deepen your relationship with God. Let us pray together:

God, for the next thirty days I am seeking you like never before. I expect to hear from you, and experience you in a magnificent way. I invite your Holy presence into this process. Let the next thirty days be faith changing and spiritually enriching.

Hear my prayer,
In Jesus Name.
Amen.

Focus: **Forgiveness**

Why are we starting with forgiveness? Building spiritually begins with letting go of those spirits that can take us to a negative place. You cannot be truly free without the spirit of forgiveness and the letting go of experiences and grudges of the past. Mahatma Gandhi says "the weak can never forgive. Forgiveness is an attribute of the strong." Well, let's get strong.

You may have heard these words before "forgive us our trespasses as we forgive those who trespass against us." A pretty cool and famous guy said that, his name was Jesus, and we repeat these words along with others that make up the Lord's Prayer.

If you look closer, you may be surprised at what you have been asking of God. "As" is the English language equivalent to the equal sign in math. When we say "she is cute AS a flower" we are saying her level of cuteness is "equal" to that of a flower.

So when we say "forgive us our trespasses as we forgive those who trespass against us." We are saying forgive us equal to as much as we forgive others.

"As" is also a conjunction that means doing something at the same time. "I cooked the food as she watched." So the prayer is also requesting that God forgive us, while we are doing the work of forgiving other people at the same time. We are to dwell and remain in the space of forgiveness.

"Father, forgive them for they know not what they do." In his last moments, Jesus reiterates forgiveness as a key ingredient to freedom and spiritual strength. He strengthens himself on the cross by releasing any weight of anger or revenge.

We strengthen our physical bodies by picking up weights, but we strengthen our spiritual bodies by letting weights go (see Hebrews 12:1). Fitness starts with a clean heart!

Forgive Who?

If you forgive those who sin against you, your heavenly Father will forgive you. But if you refuse to forgive others, your Father will not forgive your sins. (Matthew 6:14-15, NLT)

Let's face it: forgiveness is far from easy. Who really wants to let go when someone hurts you? It is quite natural to want to hold on to the offense, rehearse it or even plot revenge. But what can stop you in your tracks when going down that line are the seemingly simple verses in Matthew 6. This forgiveness thing is basically a cycle and it goes like this: you forgive someone and God forgives you. Complete. Finished. Done. But what happens if the cycle goes the other way. You don't forgive and God doesn't forgive you. Ouch! You're stuck with your own offenses—and they are against God, your Creator and Savior.

One of the best ways to push yourself toward forgiveness is to remember that God forgives you for a great multitude of things; in fact, it's impossible to live this life without doing or thinking something wrong or that goes against God. We're prone to offend God; it's in our nature. Yet, it is in God's nature to forgive us. He wants to; He desires to; He has sent Christ as our replacement for sin (see John 3:16).

So when you're focused on the wrong that someone did to you, try changing your focus to the forgiveness God offers you for all of the wrong you have done. Then ask for God's help to let your beef go with the other person—and open your heart to receive God's forgiveness. It is a beautiful cycle.

Today's Prayer Prompt:
Lord, thank you for forgiveness; help me to forgive others.

Prayer Set:
☑ Rep 1

Today I am thankful for:
☐

My Family; My Job;
The desire to lose
weight.

Challenge Reflections:

Difficult people
like Lucinda & even
my husband sometimes.
I know I need to
lean into God & deal
w/each challenge
spiritually but
that is often easier
said than done.
My prayer is that
as I work to get
closer to God that
His wisdom & guidance
through the Holy
Spirit will become
prevalent in my life.

Dealing With Others Issues

Bear with each other and forgive one another if any of you has a grievance against someone. Forgive as the Lord forgave you.
(Colossians 3:13, NIV)

We live in a world full of humans. Yep, people who make mistakes—some big, others small; some mistakes are intentional (I don't care what they say) and others are truly mishaps or oversights or just plain ignorance. But how do you keep going when others offend you, hurt you, mess up?

The letter to the church at Colosse, which is the book of Colossians, is all about how these new Christians in Colosse should interact with each other. And in today's featured verse, Paul, the writer, tells them to basically put up with each other's issues. I think Paul is saying: hey, you're going to get into it; you're going to mess up; you're going to get on each other's nerves. That's life. But, as Christians striving to live like Christ, it's important to remember forgiveness. In fact, when you look at forgiveness as an amazing gift to you from God (which it is), then you can hopefully give out that same gift to your fellow brothers and sisters much easier.

You get forgiveness from God; you give forgiveness to others. Focus on God's forgiveness so you can release forgiveness to others. It's how we can get along.

Today's Prayer Prompt:
Lord, give me what it takes to share forgiveness with others.

Prayer Set:
☑ Rep 1

Today I am thankful for:
☑ A team atmosphere in the office; God's grace & mercy that is new every a.m.; that I have the $ to get my car fixed; that we were approved to refinance our house.

Challenge Reflections:
Some slight anger resentment toward Rev. Sandy; complaining about God's blessings; health issues; a lack of sleep.

Forgive How Many Times?

> *Be alert. If you see your friend going wrong, correct him. If he responds, forgive him. Even if it's personal against you and repeated seven times through the day, and seven times he says, 'I'm sorry, I won't do it again,' forgive him. (Luke 17:3-4, MSG)*

According to Jesus' word: we are our brother and sister's keeper! In other words, if I see a brother doing wrong, I shouldn't just watch him go down that road and crash. I should say something. I should try to help my brother see the error of his ways before he hits the wall and crashes.

And if he does fix his behavior, then the matter is over—I should forgive him and move on. And if the action is something directly against me, guess what? Jesus commands that I still forgive him and move on. And not just one time—do it even seven times. And I believe this seven means as many times as it happens.

Remember, Peter asking Jesus this question? Jesus answered with seven times seventy-seven—or in other words, many times many times. (See Matthew 18:21-35).

I don't think Jesus is advocating for continuous abuse from our brother or sister—get hit as many times as possible and still pretend like nothing happened. No, I think Jesus is advocating for the spirit of forgiveness. He doesn't limit the amount of forgiveness he dishes out to us. In fact, Psalm 103:12 says he removes our sins away from us as far as the east is from the west. And as followers of Christ, we should strive to embody the same spirit as Christ.

So while no one is expected to enable an abuser, we are expected to let grievances go—just as Jesus does for us. I forgive because I want to be forgiven.

Today's Prayer Prompt:
I am my brother and sister's keeper.

Prayer Set:
☐ Rep 1

Today I am thankful for:
☐

_____

_____

_____

_____

_____

_____

Challenge Reflections:

_____

_____

_____

_____

_____

_____

_____

_____

Challenge Day 4

Be Kind

Get rid of all bitterness, rage and anger, brawling and slander,
along with every form of malice. Be kind and compassionate to
one another, forgiving each other, just as in Christ God forgave you.
(Ephesians 4:31-32, NIV)

Get rid of all bitterness, rage and anger, brawling and slander, along with every form of malice. Be kind and compassionate to one another, forgiving each other, just as in Christ God forgave you. (Ephesians 4:31-32, NIV)

There's apparently nothing new under the sun. Look at the words in today's scriptures that also come from a letter Paul wrote to early Christians—those who had just recently confessed their belief in Jesus and desire to follow in His way. Yet, right in the middle of a letter, Paul felt the need to share with the Ephesians that they needed to get rid of bitterness, rage and anger. They had some hot fights. They were brawling and slandering—lying on each other—and just downright ugly to each other.

Have you ever been in this type of environment? Perhaps at work or at home or even at church. People just can't get along or always trying to push their own agenda or pitting others against each other. It doesn't look a lot like Christ. And it's not.

Instead as Christians, we should strive to be kind and compassionate with each other. And truly the only way to do this is to be quick to forgive offenses. As we mature in Christ—go deeper and get spiritually fit—forgiveness is a big part of our growth. The quicker we are to forgive, the sooner we can begin looking more like Christ, the sooner we can treat each other with kindness and compassion. Why? Because we're not focused on offenses; rather, we are grateful for the forgiveness we consistently receive from Christ and can extend that same grace and forgiveness to others. Conflict and confusion—offenses and bruises—give us a chance to practice our forgiveness, lift another weight, and become stronger. Are you looking more like Christ these days?

Today's Prayer Prompt:
Be quick to forgive offenses.

Prayer Set:
☐ Rep 1

Today I am thankful for:
☐

_____

_____

_____

_____

_____

Challenge Reflections:

_____

_____

_____

_____

_____

_____

Challenge Day

5

You're New

*This means that anyone who belongs to Christ has become
a new person. The old life is gone; a new life has begun!*
(2 Corinthians 5:17, NLT)

Let's face it—forgiveness is not the easiest thing to do. Your mind wants to rehearse what happened; you want to pick up the phone and share with a friend what happened. You've got a few things you want to say to that person who offended you too. It's just usually not your first thought to forgive the person and move on.

But when we have accepted Christ as our savior, we are different. Our change may not occur over night, but the more we continue on this Christian journey, strengthening our faith through God's word, prayer, and other spiritual disciplines, we shed our old skin—much like a moth turning into a butterfly. A new creature, a new person with a new heart begins to emerge. And it is a glorious sight to behold.

On this journey to get spiritually fit, it may sometimes seem rough, as if you're not changing quick enough. But you are definitely changing. Take time to review how you handle some situations and compare your actions to things you would have done a month ago, a year ago or earlier. Can you see how you've grown? Are you becoming more like Christ? Taking on more and more characteristics of our savior? Have you let some things go—choosing to forgive rather than simmer in anger?

Remember, slow progress is still progress. Rejoice in your growth. Rejoice in the new life God has given you. You are not the same. You are a new creation. Fly, butterfly.

Today's Prayer Prompt:
I am a new creation.

Prayer Set:
☐ Rep 1

Today I am thankful for:
☐

Challenge Reflections:

How Does Love Look?

Love is patient, love is kind. It does not envy, it does not boast, it is not proud. It does not dishonor others, it is not self-seeking, it is not easily angered, it keeps no record of wrongs.
(1 Corinthians 13:4-5, NIV)

Love is patient, love is kind. It does not envy, it does not boast, it is not proud. It does not dishonor others, it is not self-seeking, it is not easily angered, it keeps no record of wrongs. (1 Corinthians 13:4-5, NIV)

The heart of the gospel message is centered around a four-letter word: Love. It is love that made God send Christ to earth as a sacrifice for our sins. It is love that prompted Christ to follow through with the greatest act of service—just for us. And so, it is this same love that Christians should embody to identify ourselves as followers of Christ. But it is not an emotional, mushy, red heart-shaped emoji type of love; the love of Christ looks more like the description in today's verse.

Love seeks to be patient with others, recognizing they may be on this journey at a slower pace than we are; it does not get impatient or aggravated so quickly. Love is also kind, a simple pureness that comes from being aligned with God's spirit. Love doesn't envy what others have nor does it boast about what we have. Love doesn't keep that kind of score. Love isn't about self. It really is about others—loving others as we love ourselves, trying to love others as God has so freely loved us.

When we consider God's love for us—it can be overwhelming and joyous all at the same time. And, it should be a reminder to strive to love others the same way—fully and without conditions

Today's Prayer Prompt:
Go out and show love today.

Prayer Set:
☐ Rep 1

Today I am thankful for:
☐

Challenge Reflections:

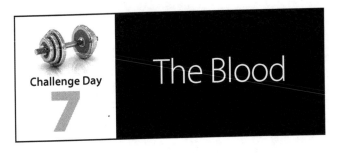

Challenge Day

7

The Blood

This is my blood of the covenant, which is poured out for many for the forgiveness of sins. (Matthew 26:28, NIV)

Most Christians repeat these words at least monthly, if not weekly, when we participate in communion, or the remembrance of the Lord's Last Supper. The pastor or the officiant serving the bread and wine might hold up a cup and proclaim these words. If you really listen to them and embody them, they probably will give you chills—every time.

Reread the words aloud now. Remember, these are Jesus' words, the words He utters the night before He is led to the cross to be crucified. These are the words He leaves with His disciples (and present-day followers like us) right before He completes His very mission for coming to earth. Jesus, fully aware of all He will endure just for us, reminds us that this drink, this wine, this grape juice is a symbol of His blood. And His precious blood will be poured out for the forgiveness of our sins.

He is the ultimate sacrifice. His death was in place of our sins. So we wouldn't have to pay the penalty for our sins, He died. And that's what the wine symbolizes. We shall never forget. So when you struggle with forgiveness, think about the blood, poured out feely for you. The blood is at the center of Christianity—it symbolizes just how much God loves us and how far He was willing to go for us.

Today's Prayer Prompt:
Thank God for the blood.

Prayer Set:
☐ Rep 1

Today I am thankful for:
☐

Challenge Reflections:

Focus: **Trust**

If you were raised like me, you probably heard the phrase: "because I told you so" plenty of times.

"Mama, why do I have to eat my vegetables?"

"Because I told you so."

"Mama, why do I have to pick up my room or wash the dishes?"

"Because I told you so."

While this phrase may have gotten on your last nerve (like it did mine), if you look deeper at it, you might be able to see a principle needed in this spiritual training, in this quest to go deeper in our relationship with Christ.

You see, what my mama really was saying is do whatever it is I told you to do, not because I'm a tyrant and I want to control you, or not because I'm too tired to explain things (although this might have been true too). Mama was saying to do what I said do and acquiesce simply because of our relationship. In other words, Mama said: you don't need to understand in order to obey, only know I have your best interest at heart.

Mama was trying to remind us that understanding is not the prerequisite to obedience. And if we would carry that golden nugget into our spiritual relationship, we'd obey God more readily. If God says to do something, we should do it—regardless of our understanding or not. And we don't just do these things blindly because we don't have minds. We do them because we do have minds, and we can use our minds to recall that God loves us, God wants the best for us, God has plans to make us happy and prosperous (see Jeremiah 29:11). God, just like our mother although in a bigger way, is not trying to hurt us. And based on our relationship with God, we can trust Him and do whatever He says. No questions asked.

The reality is you cannot bring a finite human mind to an omniscient infinite God and expect to understand the explanations of an omniscient God to a finite mind. If you're waiting to always understand it before you do it, you're never going to end up doing it. I truly believe there's some stuff about God you're never going to understand. I believe there's some stuff, just like your parents, that when they ask you to eat your green beans, you were too young to understand the vitamins that were in green beans and why they were necessary to healthy growth. You were too young to understand what those vitamins do to your body and how they provide certain nutrients for your neurological system and how they maintain a healthy metabolism. You didn't completely comprehend green beans. So, it did no good for your mama to explain to a five- year-old all the benefits of eating green beans. So, this is what she said, just eat your green beans.

And later on, when you got older and you took biology and you had science teachers then you began to understand that the green beans were green because they had chlorophyll in them and that the chlorophyll was part of the photosynthesis process by which carbon dioxide was being turned into oxygen, which was emitted back into the air. And that's why your mother simply said "eat your green beans."

I'm trying to push the point that trusting God comes from knowing that God has your best interest at heart. Trusting mom and trusting dad was because we knew, "They'll never hurt us."

As we move into week 2 of praying more and studying God's word more and being intentional about doing acts of kindness and attending worship, we will focus on trust. Why trust God? What does God's resume say to us personally that makes us trust Him.

We've been praying mightily and we want our prayers answered. We are continuously remembering the beauty of forgiveness and we are extending it to others. We don't want unforgiveness or ill intentions to block our prayers because we know that the prayers of the righteous (those in right standing with God) are answered. So now, we're going to do more heavy lifting to build some spiritual muscles. We're going to focus on how much we trust God—and how that trust looks in our everyday lives.

You may think that it is important for God to "hear" your prayers; and you are right. I propose that it is more important for God to see your obedience and righteousness. And how does he see them? Through your actions.

Is He seeing a fervent desire to live a good life, to not hurt people, to not abuse people, to love thy neighbor as thyself, to go out of our way for people's needs? Is He seeing somebody who if they had two tunics would take one tunic off their back and give it to their brothers or sisters? Is he seeing something that says that you are real about this thing or are you just casting up an emergency prayer that is inconsistent with the rest of your life because for the last two months you've been speaking ill of others but then the minute your mother got sick, now you want to use the same mouth to go "holy, holy, holy, holy, holy thou art." When you pray, what does God see? Does he see a desire to be obedient?

Review God's Resume

Our God, did you not drive out the inhabitants of this land before your people Israel and give it forever to the descendants of Abraham your friend? (2 Chronicles 20:7, NIV)

Trusting God is not always simple. Trust in and of itself is a pretty complex subject. Basically, you are saying someone else is capable of handling something for you. Spouses need to trust each other to handle finances, take care of children, etc. Employers need to trust workers to do what they are being paid to do. Parents need to trust teachers to "handle" their kids' education—at least during the 8 hours or so they are under their charge.

And spiritually fit Christians need to trust God; we need to trust that God can handle our situations. And sometimes that is difficult to do. But, if we take a page from Jehoshaphat, King of Israel, in today's scripture verse, we can be a step closer to trusting our God.

Jehoshaphat was faced with trouble. He was facing a war (see 2 Chronicles 20:1-2). But instead of relying on his army and his strategy, Jehoshaphat said: I must inquire of the Lord! Let me go straight to my source and get some clarity.

So the king went to the temple and prayed. Look at how he prayers. He's bold and in God's face. He reminds God of all he has done for the people of Israel. He basically runs down God's resume.

Now you may think that God is already well aware of all He's done for Israel so why does Jehoshaphat have to repeat all of this in his prayer. I think it's because Jehoshaphat isn't reminding God of His resume, Jehoshaphat is reminding himself (and his people). Sometimes when we pray, we have to recall all of the Lord's benefits, run down just what God has done for us personally (as well as collectively as a people and/or as a family). Prayer is not just about asking God for what we need; prayer puts us in a position to remember what God has already done.

When you're facing trouble, try praying and acknowledging what God has already done for you. It will get your mind ready to trust God again.

Today's Prayer Prompt:
Review God's resume for your life today.

Prayer Set:
☐ Rep 1   ☐ Rep 2

Today I am thankful for:
☐

_____

_____

_____

_____

Challenge Reflections:

_____

_____

_____

_____

_____

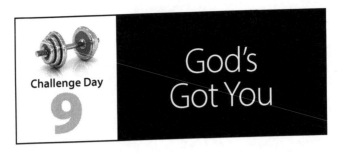

God's Got You

This is my command—be strong and courageous! Do not be afraid or discouraged. For the LORD your God is with you wherever you go. (Joshua 1:9 NLT)

Building our trust in God not only takes us reviewing God's resume for what God has done in our own lives, it also takes us remembering what God has done in others' lives too. And Joshua's story is a good one to review when looking to increase our trust muscles.

You remember, Joshua was the young man God chose to follow Moses when leading the children of Israel into the Promise Land. Joshua's assignment wasn't easy. First, he was following in the shoes of Moses, the original liberator; the one the people had followed for many years as God used him to bring Israel from the oppressive hand of the Egyptians across the Red Sea and through the wilderness. Moses was the man. He had given the people the law, or the 10 Commandments. He had been there when God rained down manna to show the people that God was a provider. Moses was right there when the cloud of fire guided the people through the night. These people knew Moses and they trusted him. But now what?

Moses was dead and the people still had to journey to the Promised Land. How would Joshua take his place? I know Joshua had to be fearful, wondering how in the world he'd handle such a big job. But God gave him a very clear answer.

God told Joshua to be strong and courageous. God told him don't get fearful or discouraged. Why not? Because God promised to be with him—wherever he went.

On the good days, God would be there; when the people got rough and tough and started to grumble again, God would be right there.

And if God can do it for Joshua, God can do it for you. Whatever you are going through today, take heed and remember God's got you. God is right there with you.

Today's Prayer Prompt:
Acknowledge that God is right by your side.

Prayer Set:
☐ Rep 1   ☐ Rep 2

Today I am thankful for:
☐

_____

_____

_____

_____

_____

Challenge Reflections:

_____

_____

_____

_____

_____

Challenge Day

10

Trust God

And they who know Your name [who have experience and acquaintance with Your mercy] will lean on and confidently put their trust in You, for You, Lord, have not forsaken those who seek (inquire of and for) You [on the authority of God's Word and the right of their necessity]. (Psalm 9:10, AMPC)

As you focus on building your trust in God, I want to ask you to think about a serious question: has God ever forsaken you? Think back over your life, has God ever failed you or let you down? I know some things may not have worked out the way you intended in life, but has God ever not provided for you or made a different way than you expected (or wanted). If you're able to read this devotion today, apparently God woke you up this morning. You may not have everything you desire, but you are able to read this page this day. So, can you really point to a time when God has failed you?

I dare say when I look at even disappointments in my own life, I can see God working things out. I still had to endure some pain and some heartache (and some things I didn't want to go through), but God has been faithful. And because I know God is faithful, I will proclaim like the psalmist in today's verse: I will lean on and confidently put my trust in God.

In other words, I, like the Psalmist, have reviewed God's resume in my life, in the life of people in the Bible, in the life of historical people, and in the life of people I know (like my family)...and I've discovered that God is amazing. I've experienced the goodness of God. Therefore, since I have done all of that, I'm going to make a bold statement: I'm going to lean and depend on God.

As the faithful members of the church I grew up in proclaimed most Sundays, "I will trust in the Lord until I die…I'm going to stay on the battlefield until I die."

So whatever place you are in, determine to stay on the battlefield, trusting in God!

Today's Prayer Prompt:
Lean on God today.

Prayer Set:
☐ Rep 1   ☐ Rep 2

Today I am thankful for:
☐

Challenge Reflections:

Challenge Day

11

Blind Faith

For we walk by faith, not by sight
(2 Corinthians 5:7, KJV)

It's what we trust in but don't yet see that keeps us going.
(2 Corinthians 5:7, MSG)

Trust equals faith; faith that the One we have trust in will take care of things. Trust means that I believe and have faith that circumstances will work out—even though they may not seem like it right now.

Today's verse reminds us that trust is not about what we see; it means we do not walk by sight. If I can see something, I know it is there. But what happens when I can't see it? Does it mean that it is not there? No, my faith says the solution, the answer, the end result is right there—regardless of whether I see it, or especially if I don't see it.

So, faith and trust is what fuels us to keep moving in the dark, searching for the light or for the solution. We know it is there (our faith has told us so) and we act accordingly.

This blind faith—walking by trust not by what we see—is what makes us different from others. Those who don't trust in God may see death, destruction, loss, etc. While those things may very well be present in your life, you also "see" what's not there. You "see" that God is by your side; you "see" that God has promised never to leave or forsake you; you "see" all that God has done before and you use these memories to help you "see" through your current situation.

Don't let what you see with the natural eye stop you from seeing with your spiritual eyes. There's much more than meets the eye when your trust is in the King of Kings, Jehovah Jireh (provider), the Balm in Gilead, your healer.

Today's Prayer Prompt:
Use your faith and trust in God to keep going.

Prayer Set:
☐ Rep 1   ☐ Rep 2

Today I am thankful for:
☐

_____

_____

_____

_____

_____

Challenge Reflections:

_____

_____

_____

_____

_____

_____

_____

Challenge Day

12

Another Benefit of Trusting

O LORD of hosts, blessed is the one who trusts in you!
(Psalm 84:12, ESV)

It's clear that trust helps us to see the light at the end of the tunnel—even when that tunnel is very dark. But, today's scripture reminds us that there is even more benefits to trusting in God—something beyond knowing and leaning on God's resume of what He's done in our lives and others' lives before now.

Another benefit of trusting is that we are blessed Not only do we get to know that God has our back and that things are really going to turn out for good (see Romans 8:28) but we get to live in a state of happiness too. Blessed means happy. When Jesus shared the Beatitudes (see Matthew 5), he started each one off with saying that the person who behaved in a certain way was blessed.

So, when we trust, we are happy, we are blessed. That's like a cherry on top of an ice cream sundae. You're already enjoying the sweet taste of ice cream drizzled with a gooey topping like fudge or caramel or strawberry. You probably have some nuts or another type of topping sprinkled on top, but then you get a nice plump cherry to enjoy. As a kid we would say: that's sweet! And that's what we get when we trust in the Lord.

Don't you want to be blessed? To receive the cherry on top of this walk with God? Trusting God can lead to a sweet life, one filled with the assurance that God will work it out—and lead and guide you along the path, regardless of how rough that path gets.

Who are you trusting today? I sure hope it's God—so you can be blessed and happy.

Today's Prayer Prompt:
Enjoy the cherry on top of trust—be happy.

Prayer Set:
☐ Rep 1   ☐ Rep 2

Today I am thankful for:
☐

Challenge Reflections:

Key to Life

Trust in the LORD with all your heart; do not depend on your own understanding. Seek his will in all you do, and he will show you which path to take. (Proverbs 3:5-6, NLT)

Most people I know are looking for the key to life—they want to know how to enjoy this life and live it the best they can. I've found that key and it is wrapped right in the center of today's verse.

To live a good life—I recommend trusting God. And the scripture says to trust with all of your heart. I don't recommend trusting God a little bit. That's like dipping your toe in the pool. You feel the coolness, but you don't get the full impact. Try jumping in and you will experience the cool water all over your body and the sensation of the relaxing and rejuvenating power of water. It's no wonder Jesus compares himself to water. When we jump in—fully trust our Lord—we too can experience in the spiritual realm the equivalent of physically jumping in a pool on a hot day.

So if you need any convincing, I recommend you use these verses as your keys. Forget relying on what you think you know—you don't and it is okay. What you need to know is the One who holds the key to your life. When you turn to Him in prayer (that's seeking his will), He will show you which way to go.

God has a path planned for each and every one of us. If we truly want to live the best life we can, we will joyously follow that path—even when we don't understand it or especially when we don't understand it. Trust makes us yield to God. Trust makes us seek God. Trust says, just as Jesus did on the cross: not my will, but yours. (see Mark 14:36)

Want to enjoy life? Jump in and trust God with all you've got. He won't let you down.

Today's Prayer Prompt:
Trust God fully.

Prayer Set:
☐ Rep 1   ☐ Rep 2

Today I am thankful for:
☐

Challenge Reflections:

When You Are Troubled

Don't let your hearts be troubled. Trust in God, and trust also in me.
(John 14:1, NLT)

God's Word really does have a prescription for everything that ails us. If we read and search the scriptures, we will find what we need. If your heart hurts—for whatever reason—I recommend you take Jesus' advice to his disciples (and to followers today) that you don't let your heart worry or be filled with sorrow.

Jesus knew sorrow. In fact, when he said the words in today's scriptures, he was facing his death. He was at the Passover meal, the last meal he ate while on earth, and he was preparing His disciples for what was to come. (I love how Jesus cared so deeply for them that He didn't leave them hanging while he ran off to take care of God's mission!) When Jesus was describing what would happen, the disciples couldn't take it. Peter wanted to fight (a human reaction to pain) and even die for Jesus (see John 13:37).

When we go through pain, we naturally react as humans. We may want to lash out or retreat or even die, and that's where Jesus serves us our much needed medicine. He says: Don't be troubled, my children. No, instead, trust in God and trust in Me.

Awww, the Balm in Gilead speaks and offers healing for our soul. When we are pained, when we face trouble, when the road ahead is so dark we can't see in front of us, we do not have to grieve like those without hope. We don't have to act as if all hope is gone. No, we can pull out God's resume, review all that He has done in the past, put on spiritual glasses to see what is not in front of us—and trust.

When you want to go deeper, build your trust in God. He will lead you on your journey.

Today's Prayer Prompt:
Go deeper—trust God.

Prayer Set:
☐ Rep 1   ☐ Rep 2

Today I am thankful for:
☐

_____

_____

_____

_____

_____

Challenge Reflections:

_____

_____

_____

_____

_____

_____

Focus: Obedience

Obedience is closely akin to trust. It is the follow up to trusting. If we say we trust God, we should have no problem obeying God. Remember the green beans. We obey mother because we trust her.

In 2 Chronicles Chapter 20 the Israelites were in quite a pickle. Three nations had formed an alliance to attack them. The attack came at an unsuspecting time and geographically from an unexpected direction. There is nothing worse than surprise trouble!

What I love most about King Jehosophat's prayer is that he did not do what most of us have a tendency to do. Our inclination is to take our solution to God and ask God to bless our solution. "Lord, please do A, B and C for me and everything will be alright." Unfortunately, this limits God because now it is a yes or no to OUR solution. The problem with this line of thinking is that God can do more than we can think or imagine (see Ephesians 3:20), which means there are solutions that God has that we will not and cannot think of and more than likely will not imagine.

Allow me to push this further. If we were trapped at the Red Sea as Moses was, and Pharoah's army was in hot pursuit, our prayer would more than likely be for weapons to fight Pharoah's army or horses to run or something of this nature. I am certain our prayer would not be, please part the sea, let us walk across, then use the water to destroy the pursuing army. That's definitely a God solution and one that would've been missed if left up to us.

Fortunately, King Jehosophat does not offer a solution, he simply says he does not know what to do, but his eyes are upon the Lord. He is open to God's solutions and ready to obey. God gives a solution, they obey and victory is won.

Take the brakes off of God and quit trying to fix it yourself. Instead of offering your solutions to God, invite God into your circumstance and watch God solve things in ways you would never imagine. Most importantly, when He answers, be ready to obey.

God's Promise

*The LORD will establish you as his holy people, as he promised
you on oath, if you keep the commands of the LORD your God
and walk in obedience to him. (Deuteronomy 28:9, NIV)*

As God fashioned the Jewish people, His chosen ones, he
made many promises to them. It started with his promise
to Abram in Genesis 12 when God said he would make a
great nation out of Abraham's descendants. And even when
trouble arose and this group of people, the Israelites, were
enslaved by the Egyptians, God heard their cries, sent Moses
to liberate them and lead them into the land God promised
them.

Today's verse shares what God spoke to the people through
Moses just before they were about to walk into the promised
land, after wandering in the wilderness for many years. God
wanted to remind the people that he had not forgotten His
promise to make the Israelites a special and holy nation. And
God also wanted to remind the people of their end of the
deal, their part of the covenant. They were to obey God and
to keep all of the commands he had given them.

As God's people, Christians who have been adopted into
God's family, we too have an obligation like the Israelites. God
will take care of us; God will keep all of his promises to us. And
we, our part, is to obey, to follow where He leads us and to
do just as He says.

You're ready to go deeper into your relationship with God? How well are you obeying His commandments? Are you living as His word directs and guides you? Obedience is key to staying spiritually fit.

Today's Prayer Prompt:
Lord, help me to obey.

Prayer Set:
☐ Rep 1　　☐ Rep 2　　☐ Rep 3

Today I am thankful for:
☐

_____

_____

_____

_____

_____

_____

Challenge Reflections:

_____

_____

_____

_____

_____

_____

_____

Love Equals Obedience

If you love me, obey my commandments.
(John 14:15, NLT)

When Jesus was preparing his disciples for his death, he shared a golden nugget with them. When the disciples were all concerned about what Jesus was saying and what would eventually happen to their beloved teacher they had followed for nearly 3 years, Jesus told them not to worry. But as they were making commitment statements, sharing how much they loved the Lord and all they were willing to do to stop him from having to suffer, Jesus said a simple statement packed with amazing power. He said: If you love me, do what I said to do.

I can imagine Jesus saying: all that undying love language promising to do this and to do that, wanting to come to the cross with me and take care of any of my enemies, that's nice. But what I really need from each of you is to do as I say. Follow My teachings. Act like I taught you during this time on Earth. Treat poeple like I treated them, show compassion and show this love you have for Me by doing what I said to do.

When we love so deeply, we do want to profess our love and even prove our love for others. We want to say just how far we'd go for another. But true love, the love Jesus was talking about, is about action. And that action is in the form of obedience.

I can tell how much you love God by how much you obey God. Jesus said it. And it's pretty simple. Love more, obey more. Love deeply, obey deeply—fully.

Today's Prayer Prompt:
Obey God fully.

Prayer Set:
☐ Rep 1   ☐ Rep 2   ☐ Rep 3

Today I am thankful for:
☐

Challenge Reflections:

Challenge Day

17

With All Your Soul

But take careful heed to do the commandment and the law which Moses the servant of the LORD commanded you, to love the LORD your God, to walk in all His ways, to keep His commandments, to hold fast to Him, and to serve Him with all your heart and with all your soul. (Joshua 22:5, NKJV)

Today's verse also comes from some of the words God gave to the Israelites—this time once they had entered into the promised land. As they were settling in, enjoying the beautiful land God had given them as an inheritance, a promsie He made to Abram, God needed to remind them again of what they were called to do, what their part of the covenant relationship would be. (Isn't it amazing how much God has to remind them—and us—of what we should do! That's why digging deeper into His word, fellowshipping regularly in church and through Bible study and prayer matters! It's a reminder of what we should be doing.)

This time God tells Joshua to tell the people to remember all of the laws God gave them through Moses—and remember to do them. He also reminds them to love God, their Lord, the one who had created them and brought them from slavery. God wanted the people to walk in the ways He had directed and to stay close to Him. Now that they were in the Promised Land, there was no time to forget their God and their covenant with Him. God reminded them to serve Him wholeheartedly and with all of their soul.

It's always interesting to me how much our journey with God paralles the Israelites' journey. Christians have a covenental relationship with God too. We have agreed to love God with all of our hearts, minds and souls because of the gift God has given us through Christ. And just as we live with the promises of God--an abundant and eternal life (see John 10:10)-- we are not to forget our covenant with our Lord. We need to stay clsoe to Him and hold fast to Him while we serve Him with our whole hearts and beings.

Don't forget about your end of the deal. Obey God always.

Today's Prayer Prompt:
Obey God always.

Prayer Set:
☐ Rep 1   ☐ Rep 2   ☐ Rep 3

Today I am thankful for:
☐

Challenge Reflections:

Challenge Day

18

Listen
and Act

Do not merely listen to the word, and so deceive yourselves.
Do what it says (James 1:22, NIV)

Don't fool yourself into thinking that you are a listener when you are anything but, letting the Word go in one ear and out the other. Act on what you hear! Those who hear and don't act are like those who glance in the mirror, walk away, and two minutes later have no idea who they are, what they look like. (James 1:22-24, MSG)

Obedience is a sign of Christian maturity. All of the praying, reading of God's Word, church attendance, worship should bear fruit—and that fruit is obedience.

As you grow deeper in your Christian walk, it should show. Not by the size of your Bible or even the amount of scripture you can recite by heart. True growth shows up in your actions. We cannot get fit by looking at weights, we have to pick them up. We cannot get spiritually fit by just listening, we have to do.

You don't just read God's word or seek to understand it, you live it. You do what God says. Not because it is easy and not even because it's what you naturally want to do; but you've grown to trust God so much that you know listening to what God says and doing it is the best thing for you—even when it may not always be the easiest thing.

I love how the Message Version translates today's scripture with an analogy. When you act on what you hear, you do not let the Word of God go in one ear and come out the other. No, obedience is more than an activity in listening. It means you take that Word to heart and follow its commands. You do as God says. Otherwise, it would be like looking in a mirror one minute and the next forgetting what you've seen. Take God's Word and carry it with you—so you can act upon it.

Today's Prayer Prompt:
Take God's Word with you—and act upon it.

Prayer Set:
☐ Rep 1   ☐ Rep 2   ☐ Rep 3

Today I am thankful for:
☐

_____

_____

_____

_____

_____

Challenge Reflections:

_____

_____

_____

_____

_____

_____

Challenge Day

19

A Special Treasure

Now if you obey me fully and keep my covenant, then
out of all nations you will be my treasured possession.
Although the whole earth is mine, (Exodus 19:5, NIV)

When obedience seems hard—or it is more tempting to walk away forgetting what God would have you to do—there's another nugget to ponder. God considers those who are obedient as a treasured possession. Knowing all God is and all God has done for you specifically, doesn't it delight you to think of yourself as a special treasure to God.

Obedience to God comes with its own set of benefits—like what is truly best for us—but the treasured possession of God adds to the benefits. Not only do I walk in God's will and according to His amazingly perfect plan for my life when I follow His word and act upon His commands, but I also get to delight God. I get to say "thank you" to my creator, my savior, my guide (and so much more) when I do what He wants me to do.

Oh, to be a treasured possession, a special gift to my God. I will follow His Word and do His will. Yes, for my benefit…but also to bring delight to my Lord.

Today's Prayer Prompt:
Obedience brings God delight.

Prayer Set:
☐ Rep 1   ☐ Rep 2   ☐ Rep 3

Today I am thankful for:
☐

_____

_____

_____

_____

_____

_____

_____

Challenge Reflections:

_____

_____

_____

_____

_____

_____

_____

_____

_____

_____

_____

Happy
Obedience

Blessed is everyone who fears the LORD,
who walks in his ways! (Psalm 128:1, ESV)

Throughout scripture, we can find many variations of today's verse. The one who follows God's commands is blessed, or happy. When we fear (reverance, hold in the highest honor) our Lord, we do exactly what He says.

How happy are you? Do you feel blessed? Are your steps being ordered by God—or is it the other way around and you're asking God to bless your steps.

Obedience looks for God and God's ways first...and then pursues them with our whole heart and mind. Obedience says my focus is on God and what He would have me to do, not the other way around.

Want more joy? More happiness? Consider your steps. Instead of trying to figure out your way, follow God. Choose obedience and you'll be blessed.

Today's Prayer Prompt:
Obey God.

Prayer Set:
☐ Rep 1   ☐ Rep 2   ☐ Rep 3

Today I am thankful for:
☐

_____

_____

_____

_____

_____

_____

Challenge Reflections:

_____

_____

_____

_____

_____

_____

_____

_____

_____

Resist Temptations

*So humble yourselves before God. Resist the devil, and he will flee
from you. Come close to God, and God will come close to you.
Wash your hands, you sinners; purify your hearts, for your loyalty
is divided between God and the world (James 4:7-8, NLT)*

When you go deeper in Christ, there's no doubt going to be some resistance. Even the devil knows that when you learn more of God, take upon His yoke and learn of Him (see Matthew 11:28-30) that you're going to gain some strong muscle and be more ready and willing to follow God. But there's a fix even for temptation. James says to resist the devil, to decide not to follow him and to refrain from listening to his temptations. And you know will happen then? The devil will flee.

Yes, growing deeper and getting spiritually fit will come with more challenges, but you've got the solution. You can resist the devil by submitting to God. You resist the devil when you refuse to follow him and turn to God, in full submission, ready and willing to be obedient to God. To humble yourself is to deny yourself. To decide to bow to God and God's ways.

When you move closer to God, God moves closer to you and continues to grant you all you need to live obediently and according to His will. When you want to please God, humbly turn toward Him as you say no to temptation...and watch and wait as God draws you closer and closer to Him, allowing you to experience the fullness of His presence.

There is beauty in God's presence. There is beauty in obeying God.

Today's Prayer Prompt:
There is beauty in obedience.

Prayer Set:
☐ Rep 1   ☐ Rep 2   ☐ Rep 3

Today I am thankful for:
☐

Challenge Reflections:

Focus: Solitude

Today we are busier than ever. We move around more than ever before. We have social media constantly bombarding us, Instagram, Facebook, Twitter, and these are just a few. We have emails, text messages, tweets, snaps, and then you have your kids always calling you. And then, no matter where you are, they can still call you.

We used to be able to leave the house and be gone or disconnected. You can't do that anymore—you'll get a text before you leave the driveway.

A recent study of 400 professionals suggested that 87% check their business email outside of work hours. Let that sink in. 87% check them outside of work hours, and 80% check their emails before they go to work. And 30% said they check their emails while still in bed in the morning, trying to make sure there are not any emergencies before they get to the office.

So think about that invasiveness. The typical work week is no longer 40 hours, but it extends into our personal lives.

And the number of monthly text messages sent has increased 7,700% over the last decade. 4.2 billion people text worldwide. 81% of Americans text regularly, and this is the one that blows my mind: 95% of text messages will be read within three minutes of them being sent. The average adult spends up to 23 hours a week texting.

We are constantly in communication with people. So is it no mystery that very few of us can remember the last time we intentionally set aside some time to be alone? And when I say alone I don't mean when you're in the car on your way to pick up someone. That's incidental solitude. I'm talking about intentional solitude. Intentional solitude is what scripture says Jesus sought. Several scriptures show him intentionally moving away from the crowd to be silent, to talk with God. He also woke up early in the morning and went to pray, in solitude. Intentionally.

Scripture says Jesus would go often to be alone. And while I cannot say with certainty the exact reasons Jesus would go, I can say that His frequency suggests that it was important to his ministry; the fact that He would often go means there's something about being in solitude and sitting and being quiet, something we need to emulate.

Now I want you to catch this, because we like to think of solitude as loneliness, and that's a misconception. Solitude is a choice; I'm choosing to retreat from my calendar, from my family, and from the people around me. I'm choosing, with a high degree of intentionality, to separate myself from external influences. Solitude is not where you're alone, solitude is where you discover you're not alone.

Solitude is where you begin to tap in to who God is and what God wants from you; it's a time-out for you to talk with your coach. You know there's several reasons players call a time-out in sports. Some need a little break or rest; some need to regroup; some need to hear from the coach because you know it's too noisy in the game to hear clearly. Sometimes you need to break up the momentum because the enemy is attacking you hard and repeatedly.

Solitude can give us so much and we need to remember to exercise intentional solitude. We need to see if we're still being our genuine selves. When you slow down and breath in and out and take some time away with God, you can evaluate your life and your game plans. You can reconnect and find out who you are.

We're all influenced by people around us, but when we don't take time to catch ourselves and check ourselves every once in a while, we can find ourselves in unhealthy places where we're living a life that is more about pleasing the people around us instead of being true to who we are.

Recharging is not selfish. It's about preparing you to continue to be mother and daddy, and grandma and grandpa, for some days to come.

Solitude allows you to build what I call quiet muscles. You have to build up the ability to sit quiet, for an extended period of time, depending on who you are. And just like any other relationship, you build it by spending time alone together. Intentional solitude allows you to spend time with your Creator. If you love God, you're trying to go deeper in that relationship. You want to hang out with God, the lover of your soul. Make sure you're intentional about God! Spend some intentional solitude with God.

Challenge Day

22

Time Out

But Jesus often withdrew to the wilderness for prayer.
(Luke 5:16, NLT)

Jesus continues to be our Master Teacher; our model for living in deeper relationship with God. Jesus shows us the way--we only have to listen and follow.

Picture Jesus during his years on earth. He traveled a lot. He spent time with His disciples, preparing them for all they needed to carry out Jesus' mission, especially when He would leave earth. Jesus healed people. Jesus taught people. He had to rebuke the overly religious people. Jesus had a very busy schedule.

Yet, today's scripture says Jesus often (that's not every now and then or sometimes), Jesus often withdrew from the crowds, from the work, from the to-do-list. And why did Jesus withdraw or take a time out? During his silent moments, Jesus needed to pray.

Jesus enjoyed the communion with His father and prayed often—not just when his mama got sick or he needed a special favor. Jesus prayed often. And He didn't just send up those quick prayers as he went about his day; Jesus was intentional about seeking out God. Jesus removed himself from the crowd and from His work (even His great mission work!)

Sometimes we just need to get away—and pray. And Jesus did it more than "sometimes." We often need to get away, find a wilderness place set aside from others, and pray.

54

How often do you take time-outs to regroup and to listen to your Father's voice? Follow Jesus' example. Make time today to withdraw.

Today's Prayer Prompt:
Take time to spend alone with God.

Prayer Set:
☐ Rep 1   ☐ Rep 2   ☐ Rep 3

Today I am thankful for:
☐

Challenge Reflections:

Challenge Day

23

What Are You Thinking About?

But his delight is in the law of the LORD,
And in His law he meditates day and night .(Psalm 1:2, NKJV)

We know that our thoughts drive us. What we think about can either put us in a good mood or a bad mood. Often times, the battle complete a task is won based on our thought process. If we think we can do something, we will. If we think we can not, we will often fail before we try. Simply put: whether you think you can or you think you can't, you are right.

So, your thought life is powerful. But imagine what happens when you fill your mind with thoughts of God's Word. A part of growing deeper in your relationship with God is meditating daily and constantly on His words. When you read the Word, you digest it and you use it to nourish your soul throughout the day.

When you meditate on God's Word, you often find the answers to your concerns immediately. When worry pops up, you may recall a scritpure that reminds you to cast your cares on God. When you're tempted to feel guilty over something you've already been forgiven for, you may remember how far God separates your sins from you—because it is in the Word.

Meditatiing on God's Word can fill you with delight. Meditating on God's Word makes you want to digest even more of God's Word so you can be filled with godly thoughts not ordinary human thoughts. When you focus on God's Word day and night, you are filled. You are blessed.

Today's Prayer Prompt:
God's Word gives you joy and peace.

Prayer Set:
☐ Rep 1   ☐ Rep 2   ☐ Rep 3

Today I am thankful for:
☐

_____

_____

_____

_____

_____

_____

_____

_____

Challenge Reflections:

_____

_____

_____

_____

_____

_____

_____

_____

_____

_____

Prayer Closets

But when you pray, go into your room, close the door and pray to your Father, who is unseen. Then your Father, who sees what is done in secret, will reward you. (Matthew 6:6, NIV)

Some people often search for just the right words when they pray. They want to bring their best to God. But truthfully, God already knows what you want to say. You can be open and honest—pouring our your heart to God rather than searching for the proper words.

In fact, Jesus even instructed us to take some time, get away and pray in secret. There's time for corporate prayer, but there's also definitely time for us to just get away and pray. No one even needs to know you're praying. You can go in private, in a place others cannot see you, and pray. You can talk to God in private and alone.

And the best part of this verse is that God will see you. God knows the secret and unspoken desires of our hearts. Getting away and uttering, even if our words are not the choicest or the best, means that God can hear us and sees our desire to commune with Him. And, God will reward us. We can be rewarded for just getting away and having a little talk with our Lord. Oh, how precious to realize that God wants to spend time alone with you. Don't neglect the beautiful privilege of prayer.

Today's Prayer Prompt:
Prayer is a privilege.

Prayer Set:
☐ Rep 1   ☐ Rep 2   ☐ Rep 3

Today I am thankful for:
☐

_____

_____

_____

_____

_____

_____

_____

Challenge Reflections:

_____

_____

_____

_____

_____

_____

_____

_____

Challenge Day

25

Benefits of Prayer

Then you will call on me and come
and pray to me, and I will listen to you.
(Jeremiah 29:12, NIV)

Prayer has many benefits. As you have worked on getting spiritually fit by praying more, spending time with God, reading His word, etc., I'm sure you've observed some of the benefits of prayer.

Communion with God gets your mind ready for the woes of the world. Talking with God puts things in perspective. It often makes you recall scripture to mediate on throughout the day or throughout the battlefield. Prayer makes you remember to forgive others so that you too can be forgiven. Prayer can set the tone of your day.

To know that God is waiting to talk with you—and God is ready to listen to you—makes the privilege of prayer even better. God's listening ear is awaiting your prayer. What do you have to share with God. Can you withdraw and have a little talk with your God, your manufacturer, your Savior and friend.

God awaits to hear from you. Don't delay, get in contact with God now.

Today's Prayer Prompt:
The many benefits of prayer.

Prayer Set:
☐ Rep 1 ☐ Rep 2 ☐ Rep 3

Today I am thankful for:
☐

_____

_____

_____

_____

_____

_____

_____

Challenge Reflections:

_____

_____

_____

_____

_____

_____

_____

_____

Challenge Day

26

God Answers

I am praying to you because I know you will
answer, O God. Bend down and listen as I pray
(Psalm 17:6, NLT)

Just getting in the position of prayer can make a difference. Readying yourself to speak with God, knowing you need to call a time-out to retreat and have a talk with Jesus is the first step to reclaiming your peace and sanity.

Seasoned saints—those of us who know the beauty of a deeper relationship with God—also know the power of being in prayer position. Time-outs may seem like we're calling for a break; but in actuality, we're calling for our Savior, we are calling out to God.

Prayer is a discipline, but prayer is also our time to call out to our God and to get an answer. The psalmist in today's scripture is confident that when he prays, God hears. And God not only hears, but God answers.

We, like the psalmist, can have that same confidence. When we've developed our relationship with God, we don't wonder if He'll answer when we pray. We know He'll answer when we pray. Why? Because we have put our trust in God and we've seen Him answer our prayers before. We obediently get away and cry out to our God…and we faithfully await His answer. We know an answer is on the way.

Today's Prayer Prompt:
Wait on God's answer.

Prayer Set:
☐ Rep 1   ☐ Rep 2   ☐ Rep 3

Today I am thankful for:
☐

_____

_____

_____

_____

_____

_____

_____

Challenge Reflections:

_____

_____

_____

_____

_____

_____

_____

_____

_____

Morning Prayer

Very early in the morning, while it was still dark,
Jesus got up, left the house and went off to a solitary
place, where he prayed. (Mark 1:35, NIV)

I tend to believe that there's nothing like an early morning prayer. Scripture shows that Jesus got up before dawn to get away and pray. Before the roosters started crowing, before the people were hustling and bustling, before the coffee was on, Jesus got up and did the most important thing he could do: he talked with God.

If you've ever gotten up right before the evidence of the sun appearing, you know it feels differently than getting up with the sunrise. When you wake up before dawn, it is still dark. The house is still quiet. Even outside, you can barely hear the city life. It's the last little time of solitutde before the day begins, like a quiet before the storm. And it is peaceful. There's really not other time like it.

Waking up early to pray sets the tone for your day. You don't have the distractions of the family. You don't have the distractions of even the trains or cars outside. It's a time of pure solitude that you can use to commune with God before the noise of the day begins.

Follow Jesus' example and try spending time with God before your day begins. Enjoy a slice of solitutde with your Creator to set the tone for your day.

Today's Prayer Prompt:
Enjoy the solitutde of morning prayer.

Prayer Set:
☐ Rep 1 ☐ Rep 2 ☐ Rep 3

Today I am thankful for:
☐

_____

_____

_____

_____

_____

_____

_____

Challenge Reflections:

_____

_____

_____

_____

_____

_____

_____

_____

_____

Challenge Day

28

Be Faithful

Be joyful in hope,
patient in affliction,
faithful in prayer.
(Romans 12:12, NIV)

If you're looking for a formular to live this Christian life, perhaps today's scripture in Romans can be a good one to follow.

The first part of the formula tells us to be joyful in hope—putting our trust in God is reason to be joyful. Whatever we are waiting for, wishing for, hoping for, we can have joy during this time.

And when we suffer, we can have patience. When our souls are afflicted, we can patiently wait for God to turn things around. Even in the midst of the storm, we can joyfully hope for better and patiently endure what we need to in order to get to the other side.

And lastly, we can be faithful in prayer. That means to pray without ceasing. To pray when things are good and to pray when things are bad. We should consistently and faithfuly submit our concerns to God, share our joys with God, and commit to communing regularly with our Lord. It's the one thing we should do constantly.

How's your prayer life?

Today's Prayer Prompt:
Faithful prayer.

Prayer Set:
☐ Rep 1   ☐ Rep 2   ☐ Rep 3

Today I am thankful for:
☐

_____

_____

_____

_____

_____

_____

_____

Challenge Reflections:

_____

_____

_____

_____

_____

_____

_____

_____

_____

Challenge Day

29

Holy Spirit Led

When the day of Pentecost came, they were all together in one place. Suddenly a sound like the blowing of a violent wind came from heaven and filled the whole house where they were sitting. They saw what seemed to be tongues of fire that separated and came to rest on each of them. All of them were filled with the Holy Spirit and began to speak in other tongues as the Spirit enabled them. (Acts 2:1-4, NIV)

The day of Pentecost marks 50 days after the Passover where Jesus had his last meal with the disciples. It is a day filled with promise. It is the day God sent the Holy Spirit, which was promised by Jesus before He left earth, to dwell with the followers.

While Jesus' death had been a sorrowful time, the resurrection of Christ brought hope and joy. It also still left a void in the followers lives. They had been used to seeing and touching Jesus, following Him and witnessing his miracles and teachings. Now that Jesus had ascended into Heaven, they were left without His physical presence.

Yet, Jesus had already said He would send the Holy Spirit (Luke 24:49) to give the people power and comfort. And now the day of Pentecost had come. And what a mighty day it was.

People from different nationalities were gathered in one place and they spoke in tongues—as the Holy Spirit guided them. All kinds of languages were heard that day—and each person heard his/her native language (see vv. 7-8). The Spirit can do that. And it's the same spirit available to us today—we just have to follow God's leading as He indwells in us.

Don't go through this Christian journey without receiving the Spirit that Jesus promised. And don't go through this journey not listening to that indewlling. God's Spirt is ready and willing to live inside of you and guide you every step of the way. Your job is to listen...and follow.

Today's Prayer Prompt:
Be ready to follow the Spirit of God.

Prayer Set:
☐ Rep 1   ☐ Rep 2   ☐ Rep 3

Today I am thankful for:
☐

Challenge Reflections:

Challenge Day

30

Purpose

"The Spirit of the LORD is upon me,
for he has anointed me to bring Good News to the poor.
He has sent me to proclaim that captives will be released,
that the blind will see, that the oppressed will be set free,
and that the time of the LORD's favor has come.
(Luke 4:18-19, NLT)

Finding our purpose has seemingly become popular these days; it is one of those buzz words we hear often. And while I believe God has gifted each of us with special skills and passions, I also believe, as Christians, our purpose is rooted in the final verses we study as we grow deeper into God.

These are the very words Jesus spoke when He stood in the temple in His hometown. He read from Isaiah and embodied the words that described His mission—and each Christian's purpose.

Can't you see Jesus, standing tall and proclaing that He has come with good news; that He will set people free and give sight to the blind. Can you hear Jesus say He will break the chains of oppression and liberate people from mental, physical and spiritual bondage? And that the time has come for His purpose to be in place.

Now, reread those words and hear your purpose. You are called to follow Jesus' footsteps and share the good news with others. You, God's child, are called to help those who are in bondage get free—including yourself. Whatever that bondage may be, you have been given the keys to unlock the chains and the controlling mechanisms.

Are you walking in your purpose? Do you take your mission seriously—every day not just on Sundays? How has God called you to use your special gifts and tools to fulfill His great purpose.

Going deeper yields new opportunities, new levels and new revelations. I pray God's amazing Spirit will guide you to new depths as you obediently follow. Look for opportunities to live out your purpose, to be free in God's truth and to share liberation with others.

Go out and live your life on purpose.

Today's Prayer Prompt:
Living purposefully.

Prayer Set:
☐ Rep 1   ☐ Rep 2   ☐ Rep 3

Today I am thankful for:
☐

Challenge Reflections:

The Cool Down

Congratulations! I pray that you have found this process to be spiritually enriching and life changing. I pray you may have learned something about yourself that will allow you to focus on your spiritual walk for years to come.

Most importantly, no matter how well you did, always stay encouraged. The hope is that you will continue to follow your spiritual fit regiment flawlessly, but any athlete will tell you, we slip sometimes. It happens. But, we head back to the gym and get right back in. Do the same for your spiritual walk. If you forget to pray or miss a devotion, hell and damnation will come upon you (ha ha ha, just kidding). Seriously, get up the next day and head back to staying spiritually fit! God always knows our hearts.

May God continue to bless you real good!

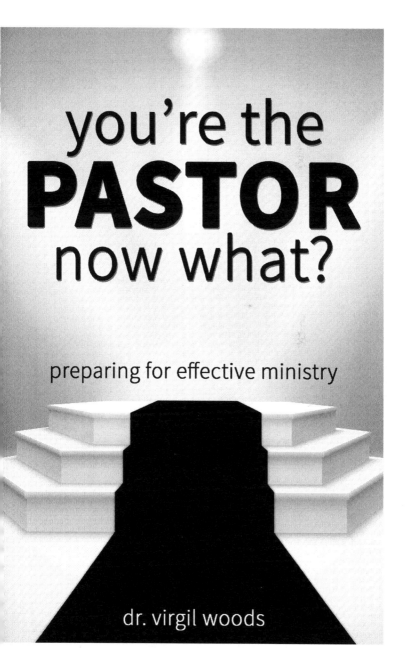

you're the
PASTOR
now what?

preparing for effective ministry

dr. virgil woods

Another great book to consider for your library

think like a fish

a fish

Seeing your Church through
the eyes of the
Unchurched

WORKBOOK
INCLUDED

dr. virgil m. woods

Made in the USA
Lexington, KY
29 January 2018